TWENTY LITTLE
PATCHWORK QUILTS

With Full-Size Templates

by

Gwen Marston and

Joe Cunningham

DOVER PUBLICATIONS, INC.
New York

This book of small quilts is
dedicated to Joe's mother, Jan Cunningham,
who was making quilts when he was small.

CREDITS

All quilts designed and made by Gwen Marston and Joe Cunningham.
All drawings by Gwen Marston and Joe Cunningham.
All photographs by The KEVA Partnership.

Twenty Little Patchwork Quilts: With Full-Size Templates is a new work, first published by Dover Publications, Inc., in 1990.

Manufactured in the United States of America
Dover Publications, Inc., 31 East 2nd Street, Mineola, N.Y. 11501

Library of Congress Cataloging-in-Publication Data

Marston, Gwen.
    Twenty little patchwork quilts.

    (Dover needlework series)
    1. Patchwork—Patterns. 2. Patchwork quilts. I. Cunningham, Joe. II. Title. III. Series.
TT835.M3783   1990   746.9′7041   89-26007
ISBN 0-486-26131-X

INTRODUCTION

In 1988 we began working on a new collection of small quilts with two goals in mind: first, to make simple, small quilts that would be easy for beginners, yet satisfying to experienced quilters, and, second, to use these quilts and others in a traveling exhibit for Northern Michigan art centers. The twenty quilts in this book are part of that exhibit.

Of these quilts, only Gwen's Tulip is an original design. We adapted The Girls from a quilt made by the late Phyllis Ashcroft and quilted by Marion Fields, both of Decker, Michigan. We would like to thank Marion for giving us permission to use the pattern here. The rest of the quilts are traditional patterns from various sources.

Whatever the original source of the pattern, we made all of the quilts in our own style, using the kinds of fabrics, sets and borders we like. As you use these patterns, we hope you will feel free to do the same. The object of quiltmaking, after all, is to be joyful and expressive, not to laboriously try to match someone else's example. Accordingly, we have not specified colors for the patterns. You can look at the pictures on the covers to see the colors we used, but we feel it is best for you to choose your own. That, after all, is one of the chief pleasures of quiltmaking.

If you are a beginning quiltmaker, working on these small quilts will teach you most of the skills you will need for larger quilts, without being intimidating. You can use scraps you already have, or start with small pieces of new fabric.

If you are an experienced quilter, you can work these up quickly to use as color or design studies for larger works.

We would also like to mention that small quilts make wonderful gifts. Making one of these for a young or old friend will probably give you as much pleasure as it gives the recipient. At least, that is what we have found.

GENERAL INSTRUCTIONS

Quiltmaking employs a number of different techniques: marking and cutting fabric, sewing pieces together, quilting and binding. None of these is particularly complicated, and we have found that anyone with a little sewing experience can learn quiltmaking easily. If you can set in a sleeve, you can piece a quilt. Here are a few ideas to guide you along, but remember, there are no hard-and-fast rules. If you need more information, your local library should have a selection of "how-to-make-a-quilt" books. Quilting and fabric stores also carry a growing number of quilt magazines and videos that provide basic instruction.

Fabric

Almost every kind of fabric has found its way into a quilt at one time or another. The great majority of quilts, however, are made of cotton. It has proven to be both light and strong and, for most quilters, it is easiest to work with.

All fabrics should be washed before you use them in your quilt, not only to pre-shrink them, but also to see if the color runs. For the small amounts you will need for these quilts it is easy to hand wash the fabrics in a sink. That way you can see any running color in the water. Continue to rinse the fabric until the water is clear. Once the fabric is washed and dried, cut off the selvage and press the fabric flat, so it will be easy to work with.

Templates

In order to sew the blocks together properly, you must cut the pieces accurately—and the smaller the patches, the more important accuracy becomes. Accurate templates will help ensure accurate piecing. All of the pattern pieces used to make these quilts are printed on lightweight cardboard at the back of the book. These templates can be cut out of the book and traced directly onto the fabric. If you piece by hand you can simply cut out the templates and use them as they are. If you piece on the machine you must add an accurate ¼″ seam allowance around each pattern piece before cutting it out. We have left room between the templates for you to do this.

To make your templates even more durable, glue the pages to another sheet of lightweight cardboard before cutting, or trace the templates onto translucent plastic.

Marking and Cutting the Patches

Each pattern piece has an arrow printed on it just as clothing patterns do. This arrow should be placed on the straight of the grain when tracing the template to the fabric to ensure that the outside edges of the block will be on the straight of the grain. This will help keep the quilt square as you work. If the pieces are cut on the diagonal or "bias," they will have a tendency to stretch out of shape.

Before you cut all of the pieces for your quilt, it is a good idea to make a sample block to make sure your templates are accurate. We once cut all of the pieces for a quilt without making a sample block first, only to discover that one template was wrong. We ended up with hundreds of odd-sized yellow triangles.

To trace the templates, draw around each one on the wrong side of your fabric with a sharp pencil. A regular lead pencil works for most marking; for dark fabrics we use a white or silver Berol Verithin pencil, which is available at most art or drafting supply shops, as well as many quilt stores.

We find we can accurately cut up to four layers of fabric at once. This means that we only have to mark the top layer. The only trick is to make sure the layers are pressed flat and that you have good, sharp scissors. You may wish to place a pin through the layers of each patch to secure them, but we find that if we keep the layers flat while we are cutting, few pins are necessary. Accurate cutting is especially important for machine sewing, since you will be using the edge of the fabric to guide the sewing line beneath the presser foot. Misshapen pieces will not fit together properly, and the whole sewing process will become a struggle.

Sewing

We pieced the blocks for all these quilts on the sewing machine. They could, of course, be done by hand, but our instructions here are for machine sewing.

We set our stitch length at 10 or 12 stitches to the inch. It is not necessary to backstitch the ends of the seams because you will be sewing over all the seams in another direction. The only place you need to backstitch is on the ends of the seams of the outside borders, where they could pull apart when the top is stretched for quilting.

Sewing any quilt block together involves starting with small units that can be joined together into larger units. For the red and white Four Patch, for example, first sew one red square to one white square. Repeat, then join the two units to make the complete block. All the blocks in this book can be divided into small units like this, which can be assembled along straight seams.

Mass sewing, or "chain piecing," will make your work go faster. For example, to make many four-patch blocks, begin by sewing all the red squares to white ones, one after another. Do not lift the presser foot or cut the thread between the pairs of patches. Once you have sewn them all, clip them apart. If you are sewing triangles, trim the protruding points so they won't get in your way when you are quilting. Now press the seams to one side before you continue. Whenever possible, it is best to press the seams toward the darker fabric, so the darker fabric won't show through the lighter.

Once the blocks are complete, sew them into strips of blocks, adding lattice strips if they are part of the pattern. Finally, pin the strips of blocks together, pinning the junctions carefully where the points will meet, then sew them together to complete the quilt top. All the borders for these quilts were made by first pinning and sewing the side borders, then repeating the process for the top and bottom borders.

Quilting Designs

These small quilts don't leave much room for elaborate quilting. Most of them have simple outline quilting or squares crisscrossed from corner to corner. Because of the small scale of these quilts, it is easy to outline the shapes by eye and it is not necessary to mark them. The narrow borders require simple small-scale designs. We have included some possible quilting patterns on page 48.

The quilting designs should be marked on the fabric as lightly as possible. A hard lead #3 or #4 pencil can be used; however, Berol Verithin pencils are our favorite marking pencils because they are easy to use and wash out completely. We use a silver pencil for light fabrics and a white one for dark.

Quilting patterns can be traced directly onto light fabrics, and with the aid of a light table, onto dark fabrics. If you don't have a light table, you can just pin the quilting design to the back of the quilt top and hold it up to a window for tracing. In some cases it is easier to make a cardboard template of the design.

Backing

Cut the back of your quilt about 1″ to 1½″ larger than the top on all four sides. You can use a good-quality muslin, choose one of the fabrics from your quilt top, or introduce an entirely new fabric for the back of your quilt.

Batting

We like to use a thin cotton batting in small quilts. Polyester batting seems too puffy for these small quilts . . . *to us.* You might like to experiment with several types of batting and see which appeals to you the most.

Quilting

These small quilts can be easily quilted in your lap, in a hoop or in a full-size frame. If you lap quilt or use a hoop you will need to baste the three layers together securely.

For both quilting and basting, we get the best results by stretching the quilt in a full-size frame that we make ourselves. This frame consists of four 1″ × 2″ pine boards about 36″ long. For each board, cut a strip of sturdy fabric about 5″ wide and the length of the board. Fold under about ½″ on each long edge of the fabric, then fold the strip in half lengthwise. Staple the strip to the board with the folded edge extending about ½″ over the edge (*Fig. 1*). Lay one pair of boards across the other, as in *Fig. 2,* then baste the backing to the top boards. Stretch the backing tight and secure the corners of the boards with small C-clamps. Pin

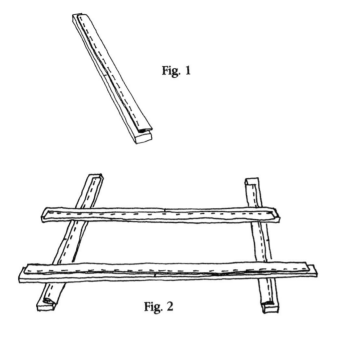

Fig. 1

Fig. 2

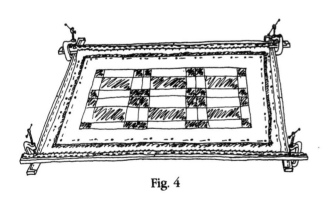

Fig. 3

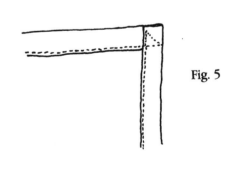

Fig. 4

The Quilting Stitch

The stitch is nothing more than a running stitch—but it is done differently than in other hand sewing. Keeping one hand underneath the frame to feel the needle, use the thimble to "rock" the needle up and down, building up four or five stitches on it before you pull it through. Short needles called "betweens" are made for just this purpose. The larger the number, the smaller the needle. We find that we prefer a #9, but quilters vary a great deal on the size of needle they like to use. Cotton quilting thread will knot and ravel less than polyester thread. We use a regular nickel silver thimble to guide the needle through the quilt.

For complete instructions on the stitch, see our book, *70 Classic Quilting Designs* (Dover 0-486-25474-7).

Finishing

An old-fashioned way to finish the edges of your quilt is to bring the backing around to the top and topstitch it. We set the stitch length on the machine to 12 to 15 stitches to the inch for a neat, tiny stitch. Trim the batting even with the edge of the top, then trim the backing so it extends ½". Fold the backing around to the top, turn the edge under ¼" and sew along the edge. Work carefully and slowly for the neatest job. A good secure corner treatment is to stitch to the very edge of one side, then sew a little triangle as you turn the corner (*Fig. 5*).

A separate binding can be cut on the straight or on the bias. An easy way to make a ¼" (finished) bias binding is to lay a yardstick at a 45° angle across your fabric and mark several 1"-wide lengths of bias. Join the strips together as shown in *Fig. 6*. Lay the binding on the top of your quilt with the right sides together and the raw edges matching. Sew it down, then turn it toward the back; turn in ¼" on the raw edge and stitch the folded edge down with a hidden stitch.

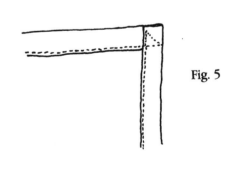

Fig. 5

the two loose edges of the backing to the frame every 1" to 2" (*Fig. 3*). Spread the batting over the backing and smooth it out. Lay the quilt top on the batting and pin around the edges (*Fig. 4*). Check to make sure it is stretched tight and that there are no wrinkles in the backing or the top. If it is smooth and wrinkle-free, you are ready to begin quilting or basting.

Fig. 6

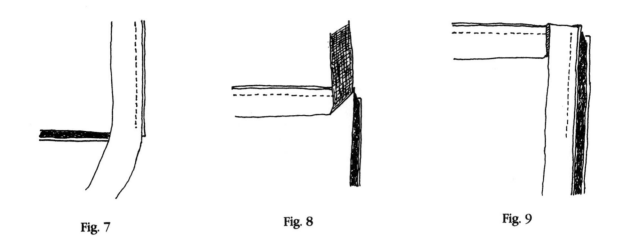

Fig. 7   Fig. 8   Fig. 9

If you want a mitered corner on the binding, sew to ¼″ from the edge of the quilt (*Fig. 7*), ending with the needle in the fabric. Lift the presser foot, turn the quilt 90° in the next direction, lift the needle out and pull the quilt toward you a few inches. Fold the bias up away from the quilt at a right angle (*Fig. 8*), then bring it straight down to form the miter.

Place the needle carefully into the quilt ¼″ in from both sides of the corner and continue sewing (*Fig. 9*). Repeat this process for all four corners. Trim away the backing and batting evenly, turn the binding to the back side and stitch down with a hidden stitch.

Now you are ready to begin your next small quilt!

HOUSES

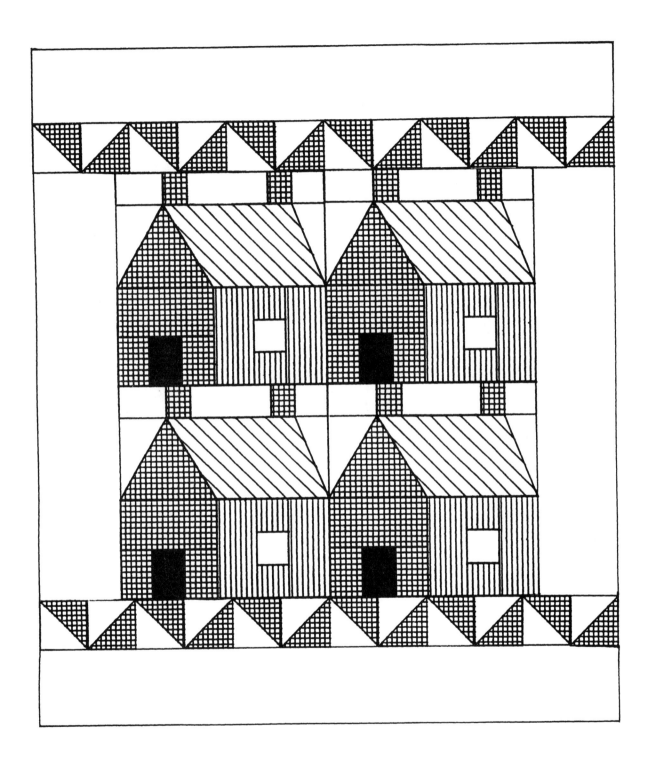

Finished size of quilt: 18½″ × 20½″.

Finished size of block: 6½″ square.

Number of blocks in quilt: Four.

Templates used: H1–H10, Y (for border).

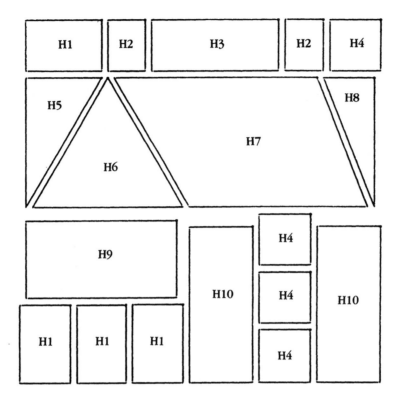

Fig. 1

Number of pieces to cut for each block:
Some templates are used for several different sections of the house (see *Fig. 1* for placement). Choose a different fabric for each section—chimneys, house front, house side, etc.

H1—two for house front, one for door and one for sky.

H2—two for chimneys.

H3—one for sky.

H4—one for sky, one for window and two for house side.

H5—one for sky.

H6—one for house front.

H7—one for roof.

H8—one for sky.

H9—one for house front.

H10—two for house side.

Side borders: Finished size, 2¾″ × 13″. Cut two strips 3″ × 13½″ of white.

Sawtooth borders: Finished size, 1½″ × 18½″. Cut 24 white and 24 dark Y triangles.

Top and bottom borders: Finished size, 2¼″ × 18½″. Cut two strips 2½″ × 18½″ of white.

Each block is constructed in three horizontal rows. For the top row, sew the H1 sky, H2 chimney, H3 sky, H2 chimney and H4 sky together to form a strip (*Fig. 2*). For the center row, sew the H5 sky, H6 house front, H7 roof and H8 sky together (*Fig. 3*). The bottom row is constructed in several steps. First, sew an H1 house front to each long edge of the H1 door (*Fig. 4*). Sew the H9 house front to the top of this piece to make a square (*Fig. 5*). Sew an H4 house side to opposite sides of the H4 window (*Fig. 6*). Sew an H10 house side to each long edge of this piece to form a square (*Fig. 7*). Sew the two squares together (*Fig. 8*). Sew the three rows together, carefully matching the seams (*Fig. 9*).

Sew two blocks together side by side. Repeat with the other two blocks. Sew the two pairs together. Sew on the side borders.

To construct the sawtooth border, first sew the white and dark Y triangles together to form squares (*Fig. 10*). Sew these squares together in pairs as in *Fig. 11*; then sew six pairs together for each border strip (*Fig. 12*). Sew a strip to the top and bottom of the quilt top. Sew the outer borders to the top and bottom edges.

Finish the quilt following the General Instructions.

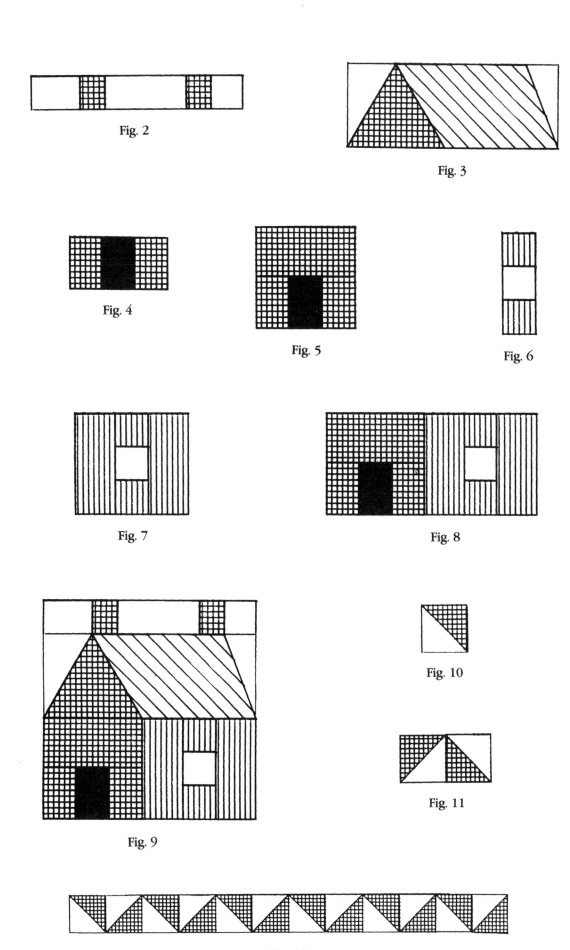

Fig. 2

Fig. 3

Fig. 4

Fig. 5

Fig. 6

Fig. 7

Fig. 8

Fig. 9

Fig. 10

Fig. 11

Fig. 12

THE GIRLS

Finished size of quilt: 15″ × 19½″.

Finished size of block: 6″ square.

Number of blocks in quilt: Four.

Number of pieces to cut for each block:
  A—four white.
  F—two white, two dark.
  M—two white, two dark.
  O—two dark.
  S—two white.
  U—one dark.

Templates used: A, F, M, O, S and U.

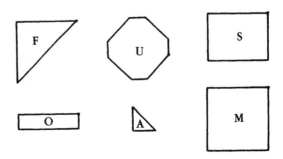

Lattice strip: Finished size, 2″ × 12″. Cut one 2½″ × 12½″ strip of white.

Side borders: Finished size, 1½″ × 14″. Cut two 1¾″ × 14½″ strips of color desired.

Top and bottom borders: Finished size, 2¾″ × 15″. Cut two 3″ × 15″ strips of color desired.

We got the idea for this quilt from one pieced by the late Phyllis Ashcroft and quilted by Marion Fields, who gave us permission to use the pattern. Marion's quilt is shown in our book *Michigan Quilts* (Michigan State University Museum, 1987).

Each block is constructed in three horizontal rows. For the first row, sew the A triangles to the corners of the U octagon to form a square (*Fig. 1*). Sew a white M square to opposite sides of the pieced square (*Fig. 2*). For the second row, sew an O "arm" strip to one side of each S rectangle (*Fig. 3*). Sew the resulting squares to opposite sides of a dark M square (*Fig. 4*). For the third row, sew the white F triangles to the dark F triangles to form squares (*Fig. 5*). Sew a pieced square to opposite sides of a dark M square to make the skirt (*Fig. 6*). Sew the rows together to complete the block (*Fig. 7*).

Sew two blocks together side by side; sew the lattice strip to the bottom edge. Sew the remaining two blocks together and sew to the free edge of the lattice strip. Sew on the side, then the top and bottom borders.

Finish the quilt following the General Instructions.

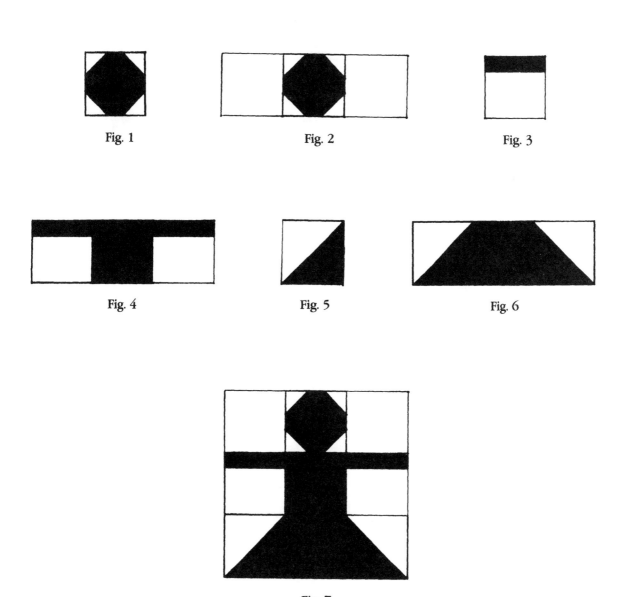

Fig. 1   Fig. 2   Fig. 3

Fig. 4   Fig. 5   Fig. 6

Fig. 7

GWEN'S TULIP

Finished size of quilt: 14½″ × 19½″.

Finished size of block: 4″ square.

Number of blocks in quilt: 12.

Number of pieces to cut for each block:
  B—four color #1, four white.
  F—two white.
  I—one color #3.
  J—two white.
  P—one color #2.

Templates used: B, F, I, J, P and L (for corner square).

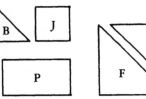
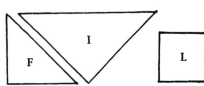

Corner square: Finished size, 1″ square. Cut six L squares of color #3.

Lattice strips: Finished size, 1″ × 4″. Cut 17 strips 1½″ × 4½″ of color desired.

This quilt is an original design by Gwen Marston.

The block is constructed in three horizontal rows. First, sew the white B triangles to the colored B triangles to form squares (*Fig. 1*). For the first row, sew two of the pieced squares together to form a rectangle as in *Fig. 2*. Sew a white J square to each end of this rectangle (*Fig. 3*). For the second row, sew a pieced square to each end of the P rectangle (*Fig. 4*). For the third row, sew an F triangle to each short edge of the I triangle to form a rectangle (*Fig. 5*). Sew the three rows together to complete the block (*Fig. 6*).

The quilt top is assembled in seven horizontal rows. For rows 1, 3, 5 and 7, sew three blocks together with lattice strips between them (*Fig. 7*). For rows 2, 4 and 6, sew three lattice strips together with corner blocks between them (*Fig. 8*). Sew the rows together, carefully matching the seams.

Finish the quilt following the General Instructions.

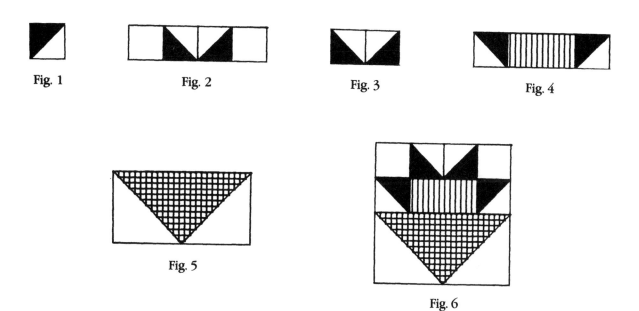

Fig. 1   Fig. 2   Fig. 3   Fig. 4

Fig. 5

Fig. 6

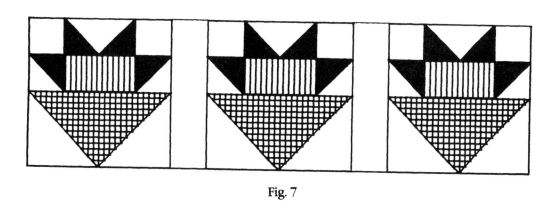

Fig. 7

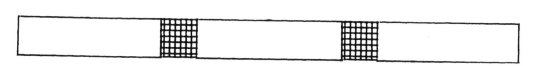

Fig. 8

LONDON STAIRS

Finished size of quilt: 17½″ × 21½″.

Finished size of block: 2″ square.

Number of blocks in quilt: 63.

Number of pieces to cut for each block:
P—one white, one dark.

Side borders: Finished size, 1¾″ × 18″. Cut two 2″ × 18½″ strips of color desired.

Top and bottom borders: Finished size, 1¾″ × 17½″. Cut two 2″ × 17½″ strips of color desired.

Sew the white rectangles to the dark rectangles to make squares (*Fig. 1*). The quilt top is assembled in nine horizontal rows of seven blocks each. The pattern is created by placing one block vertically, the next horizontally and so on.

Templates used: P.

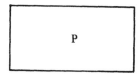

Rows 1, 3, 5, 7 and 9 begin and end with a vertical block (*Fig 2*). Rows 2, 4, 6 and 8 begin and end with a horizontal block (*Fig. 3*).

Carefully matching the seams, sew the rows together in pairs—row 1 to 2, 3 to 4, 5 to 6, etc. There will be one row left over. Sew the pairs together, adding the single row at the bottom. Sew on the side, then the top and bottom borders.

Finish the quilt following the General Instructions.

Fig. 1

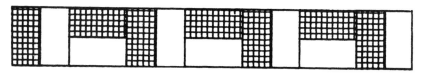

Fig. 2

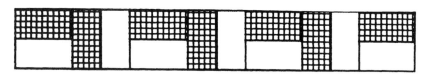

Fig. 3

PROPELLER

Finished size of quilt: 16½″ × 20½″.

Finished size of block: 5″ square.

Number of blocks in quilt: Four.

Number of pieces to cut for each block:
F—four white, four dark.
J—five white, four dark.

Templates used: F, J and B (for pinwheel square).

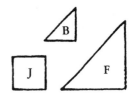

Lattice strips: Finished size, 2″ × 5″. Cut four 2½″ × 5½″ strips of white.

Pinwheel squares: Finished size, 2″ square. Cut 20 white and 20 dark B triangles.

Inner borders and side borders: Finished size, 2″ × 12″. Cut four 2½″ × 12½″ strips of white.

Outer top and bottom borders: Finished size, 2″ × 16″. Cut two 2¼″ × 16½″ strips of white.

The block is constructed in three horizontal rows. Sew the white F triangles to the dark F triangles to form squares (*Fig. 1*). For the first row, sew a white J square to a dark J square to form a rectangle (*Fig. 2*). Sew pieced squares to opposite sides of this rectangle (*Fig.*

3). For the second row, sew three white and two dark J squares together to form a strip (*Fig. 4*). Make the third row like the first. Sew the three rows together to complete the block (*Fig. 5*).

Sew the white B triangles to the dark B triangles to form squares. Sew four squares together as in *Fig. 6* for each of the five pinwheel squares.

The quilt top is assembled in three horizontal rows. For rows 1 and 3, sew a block to each side of a lattice strip (*Fig. 7*). For row 2, sew a lattice strip to opposite sides of a pinwheel square (*Fig. 8*). Sew rows 1 and 2 together, add row 3 to the lower edge. Sew on the side borders. Sew a pinwheel square to each end of the inner top and bottom borders. Sew these borders to the quilt top. Sew on the outer top and bottom borders.

Finish the quilt following the General Instructions.

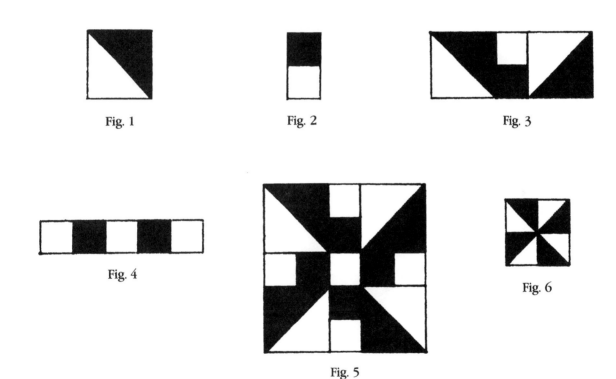

Fig. 1   Fig. 2   Fig. 3

Fig. 4

Fig. 6

Fig. 5

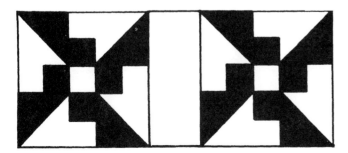

Fig. 7

Fig. 8

BOW TIE

Templates used: A, L and T.

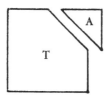

Finished size of quilt: 18½″ × 21½″.

Finished size of block: 3″ square.

Number of blocks in quilt: 20.

Number of pieces to cut for each block:
A—two color #2
L—two color #1.
T—two color #2.

Inner top and bottom borders: Finished size, 1″ × 12″. Cut two 1½″ × 12½″ strips of color desired.

Inner side borders: Finished size, 1″ × 17″. Cut two 1½″ × 17½″ strips of color desired.

Outer side borders: Finished size, 2¼″ × 17″. Cut two 2½″ × 17½″ strips of color desired.

Outer top and bottom borders: Finished size, 2¼″ × 18½″. Cut two 2½″ × 18½″ strips of color desired.

It is not necessary to make all of the blocks the same color. In our simplified version of the Bow Tie, shown in color on the inside front cover, we used several different colors for the bow ties and organized them to run in diagonal rows.

To construct each block, first sew an A triangle to a T piece as in *Fig. 1* to form a square. Sew this pieced square to a plain L square to form a rectangle (*Fig. 2*). Repeat to form a second rectangle. Sew the rectangles together to complete the block (*Fig. 3*).

Arrange the blocks in five rows of four blocks each, making sure that all of the blocks are turned in the same direction. Pin, then sew the blocks together. Sew on the inner top and bottom borders, then the inner side borders. Sew the outer side borders to the sides, then sew on the outer top and bottom borders.

Finish the quilt following the General Instructions.

Fig. 1

Fig. 2

Fig. 3

DRUNKARD'S PATH VARIATION

Finished size of quilt: 17″ × 19¾″.

Finished size of block: 2¾″ square.

Number of blocks in quilt: 42—21 of each color scheme.

Number of pieces to cut for quilt shown:
E—21 light, 21 dark.
Z—21 light, 21 dark.

To make each block, sew an E triangle to a Z piece to make a square (*Fig. 1*). Make 21 blocks each of the two color schemes shown in *Fig. 2*.

Arrange the blocks in seven rows of six blocks each, alternating the colors and making sure that all of the blocks are turned in the same direction. Rows 1, 3, 5 and 7 should begin with a dark block (*Fig. 3*); rows 2, 4

Templates used: E and Z.

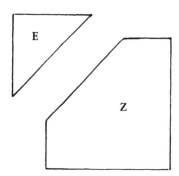

and 6 should begin with a light block (*Fig. 4*). Pin, then sew the blocks together in rows. Sew the rows together, sewing row 1 to row 2, adding 3, then 4, etc.

Finish the quilt following the General Instructions.

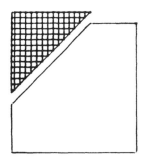

Fig. 1

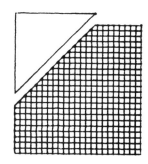

Fig. 2

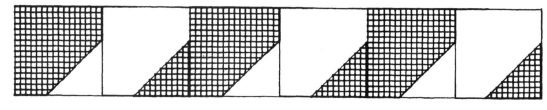

Fig. 3

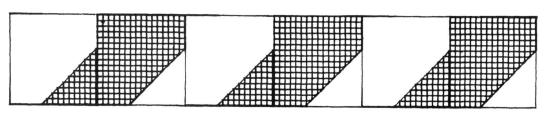

Fig. 4

ANVIL

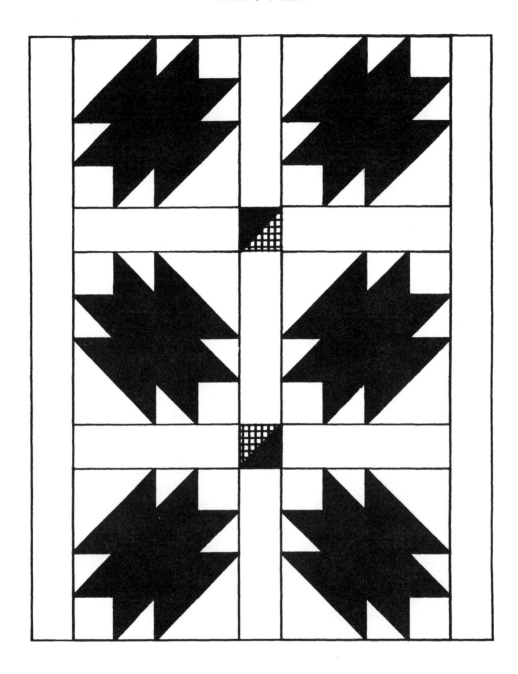

Finished size of quilt: 13¾″ × 17¾″.

Finished size of block: 5″ square.

Number of blocks in quilt: Six.

Number of pieces to cut for each block:
    C—four color #1, four color #2.
    G—two color #1, two color #2.
    K—two color #1, two color #2.

Lattice strips: Finished size, 1¼″ × 5″. Cut seven 1¾″ × 5½″ strips of color #2.

Corner squares: Finished size, 1¼″ square. Cut two C triangles from color #1 and two from color #3.

Templates used: C, G and K.

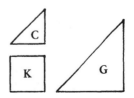

Side borders: Finished size, 1¼″ × 17¾″. Cut two 1½″ × 17¾″ strips of color #2.

To construct each block, sew the color #1 C triangles to the color #2 C triangles to form squares (*Fig. 1*). Repeat with the G triangles. Join two of the small pieced squares to two different-colored K squares as in *Fig. 2*; sew the resulting strips together to form a square. Sew this square to a large pieced square as in *Fig. 3* to form a half block. Repeat to form a second half block, then sew the two halves together to complete the block (*Fig. 4*).

To form the corner square, sew a color #1 C triangle to a color #3 triangle to form a square. Repeat to form a second corner square.

The quilt top is assembled in five horizontal rows. For row 1, sew a block to either side of a lattice strip as in *Fig. 5*. For rows 2 and 4, sew a lattice strip to opposite sides of a corner square (*Fig. 6*). For rows 3 and 5, sew a block to either side of a lattice strip as in *Fig. 7*. Sew the rows together following the full quilt diagram, carefully matching the seams. Sew the borders to the sides.

Finish the quilt following the General Instructions.

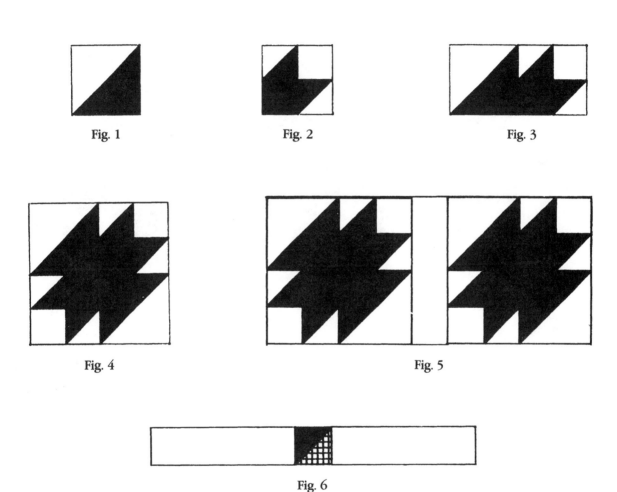

Fig. 1   Fig. 2   Fig. 3

Fig. 4   Fig. 5

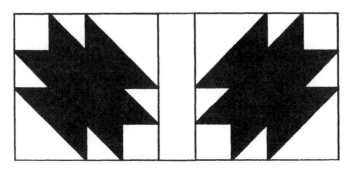

Fig. 6

Fig. 7

BROKEN DISHES

Templates used: F.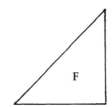

Finished size of quilt: 18″ × 22″.

Finished size of block: 4″ square.

Number of blocks in quilt: 12.

Number of pieces to cut for each block:
  F—four light, four dark.

Side borders: Finished size, 3″ × 16″. Cut two 3¼″ × 16½″ strips of color desired.

Top and bottom borders: Finished size, 3″ × 22″. Cut two 3¼″ × 22″ strips of color desired.

To construct each block, sew the light and dark triangles together in pairs to form squares (*Fig. 1*). Sew the squares together in pairs to form rectangles (*Fig. 2*), then sew the rectangles together to complete the block (*Fig. 3*).

Arrange the blocks in four rows of three blocks each, making sure that all of the blocks are turned in the same direction. Pin, then sew the blocks together. Add the side borders, then the top and bottom borders.

Finish the quilt following the General Instructions.

Fig. 1

Fig. 2

Fig. 3

SPOOLS

Finished size of quilt: 16¾″ × 20½″.

Finished size of block: 3¾″ square.

Number of blocks in quilt: 12.

Number of pieces to cut for each block:
    C—four white.
    K—two white, one color.
    X—two color.

Short lattice: Finished size, 1″ × 3¾″. Cut 11 strips
1½″ × 4¼″ of color desired.

Templates used: C, K and X.

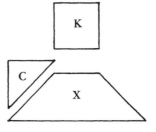

Long lattice: Finished size, 1″ × 4¾″. Cut six 1½″ × 5¼″ strips of color desired.

Side borders: Finished size, 1¾″ × 20½″. Cut two 2″ × 20½″ strips of color desired.

Top and bottom borders: Finished size, 1¼″ × 13¼″. Cut two 1½″ × 13¾″ strips of color desired.

Each block is constructed in three horizontal rows. For the first and third rows, sew a C triangle to each diagonal edge of the X piece to form a rectangle (*Fig. 1*). For the second row, sew a white K square to opposite sides of a colored K square to form a strip (*Fig. 2*). Sew the three rows together to complete the block (*Fig. 3*).

The quilt top is assembled in four rows of three blocks each. For the first row, sew a short lattice strip to the side edge of a block (*Fig. 4*), then sew a long lattice strip to the lower edge (*Fig. 5*). Repeat with a second block. Sew a short lattice strip to the lower edge of a third block (*Fig. 6*). Sew the three blocks together as in *Fig. 7*. Make two more rows the same. For the last row, sew three blocks together with short lattice strips between as in *Fig. 8*. Sew the four rows together. Sew the borders to the top and bottom, then to the sides to complete the quilt top.

Finish the quilt following the General Instructions.

The quilt shown on the inside front cover was made from feed sacks given to us by Margaret Moody of Cleveland, Ohio.

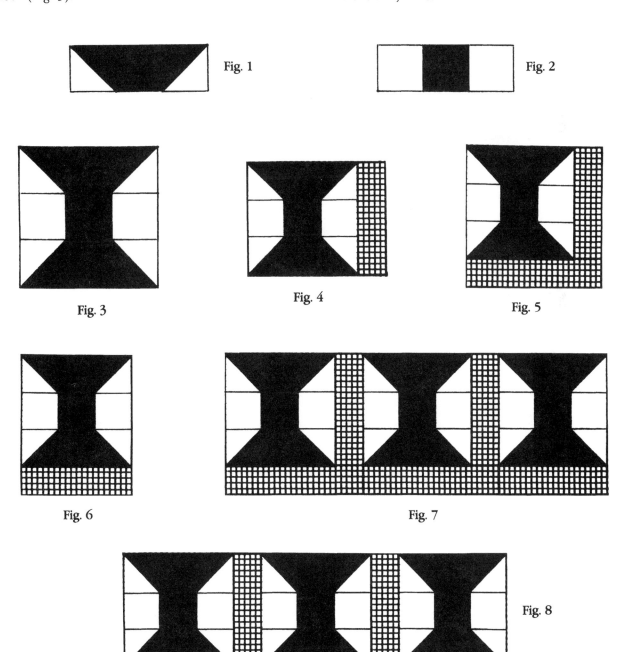

Fig. 1

Fig. 2

Fig. 3

Fig. 4

Fig. 5

Fig. 6

Fig. 7

Fig. 8

DUTCHMAN'S PUZZLE

Finished size of quilt: 14½″ × 18½″.

Finished size of block: 5″ square.

Number of blocks in quilt: Four whole blocks and two half-blocks.

Number of pieces to cut for each whole block:
   C—16 white.
   E—eight color. These do not all have to be the same.

Templates used: C, E and L (for corner squares).

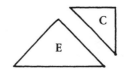

Lattice strips: Finished size, 1½″ × 5″. Cut six 2″ × 5½″ strips and one 2″ × 3″ strip of color desired.

Corner squares: Finished size, 1½″ square. Cut two of color desired, using Template L.

Side borders: Finished size, 1½″ × 15½″. Cut two 1¾″ × 16″ strips of color desired.

Top and bottom borders: Finished size, 1½″ × 14½″. Cut two 1¾″ × 14½″ strips of color desired.

First, sew two small C triangles to each E triangle to form rectangles (*Fig. 1*). Sew the rectangles together in pairs to form squares as in *Fig. 2,* then sew these squares together in pairs to form larger rectangles as in *Fig. 3.* Put aside two of these rectangles for the half-blocks. Sew the remaining rectangles together in pairs as in *Fig. 4* to complete four blocks.

The quilt top is assembled in five horizontal rows. For rows 1 and 3, sew a whole block to either side of a lattice strip (*Fig. 5*). For rows 2 and 4, sew a lattice strip to either side of an L corner square (*Fig. 6*). For row 5, sew a half-block to either side of the short lattice strips as in *Fig. 7.* Pin, then sew the rows together. Add the side borders, then the top and bottom borders.

Finish the quilt following the General Instructions.

 Fig. 1

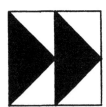 Fig. 2

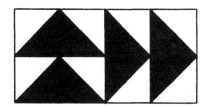 Fig. 3

Fig. 4

Fig. 5

 Fig. 6

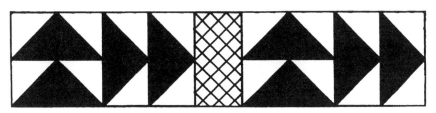 Fig. 7

WINDMILL

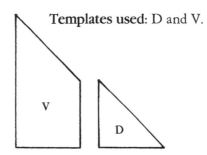

Templates used: D and V.

Finished size of quilt: 16½″ × 20½″.

Finished size of block: 4″ square.

Number of blocks in quilt: 20.

Number of pieces to cut for each block:
  D—four white.
  V—four dark.

Sew a D triangle to each V piece to form a triangle (*Fig. 1*). Sew these triangles together in pairs to form larger triangles (*Fig. 2*). Sew two large triangles together along the long edge for each block (*Fig. 3*).

Carefully matching the seamlines, sew the blocks together in five rows of four blocks each. Sew the rows together to complete the quilt top.

Finish the quilt following the General Instructions.

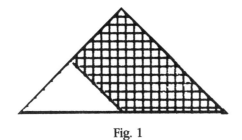

Fig. 1

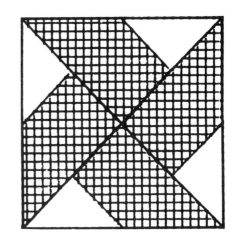

Fig. 2

Fig. 3

FOUR PATCH

Finished size of quilt: 15″ × 19″.

Finished size of block: 2″ square.

Number of blocks in quilt: 24 pieced and 24 plain.

Number of pieces to cut for each pieced block:
  J—four white, four color #1

Plain blocks: Cut 24 M squares from color #2.

Side sawtooth borders: Finished size, 1¼″ × 16″. (See cutting directions below.)

Templates used: J, M (for plain blocks) and C (for border).

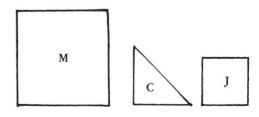

Top and bottom sawtooth borders: Finished size, 1¼″ × 15″. Cut about 56 C triangles of color #1 and 56 C triangles of color #2 for all four of the borders.

For each pieced block, sew a colored J square to a light J square to form a rectangle (*Fig. 1*). Repeat to form a second rectangle. Turning one rectangle around so that the colors are reversed, sew the rectangles together to form a square (*Fig. 2*).

The quilt top is constructed in eight rows of six blocks each, alternating the pieced and plain blocks. Rows 1, 3, 5 and 7 should begin with a plain block (*Fig. 3*); rows 2, 4, 6 and 8 should begin with a pieced block (*Fig. 4*). All of the pieced blocks should be turned so that a colored square is in the upper left-hand corner. Sew the rows together in pairs—row 1 to row 2, 3 to 4, 5 to 6 and 7 to 8. Sew the pairs together.

To construct the sawtooth borders, first sew the color #1 C triangles to the color #2 C triangles to form squares (*Fig. 5*). You will notice that the sawtooth pattern does *not* work out evenly at the corners. We just made a long strip, then cut the borders from this, ignoring the corner resolution. Sew the pieced squares together in pairs as in *Fig. 6* to form rectangles. Sew these rectangles together (*Fig. 7*) to make a long strip. From this strip, cut two strips the length of the quilt top and sew one to each side. Cut borders for the top and bottom and sew to the quilt top.

Finish the quilt following the General Instructions.

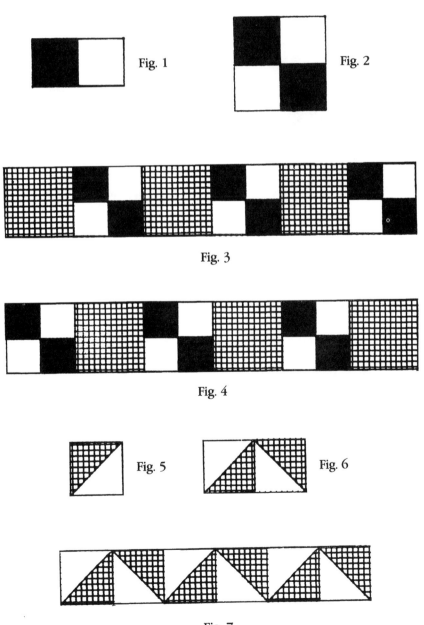

Fig. 1

Fig. 2

Fig. 3

Fig. 4

Fig. 5

Fig. 6

Fig. 7

TREE EVERLASTING

Finished size of quilt: 16½″ × 20½″.

Templates used: B.

Number of pieces to cut for quilt:
  B—120 white, 120 dark.

Bars: Cut three white and two dark 2½″ × 20½″ strips.

Sew the white and dark B triangles together in pairs to form squares (*Fig. 1*). Keeping all of the squares turned in the same direction, sew the squares together in pairs (*Fig. 2*), then sew the resulting pieces together in pairs to form 30 strips of four blocks each (*Fig. 3*). Sew five of these units together to form each 20-square strip (*Fig. 4*).

Starting at the left-hand edge of the quilt top, sew one 20-square strip to one long edge of a white bar (*Fig. 5*). Add the remaining 20-square strips and plain bars following the full quilt diagram.

Finish the quilt following the General Instructions.

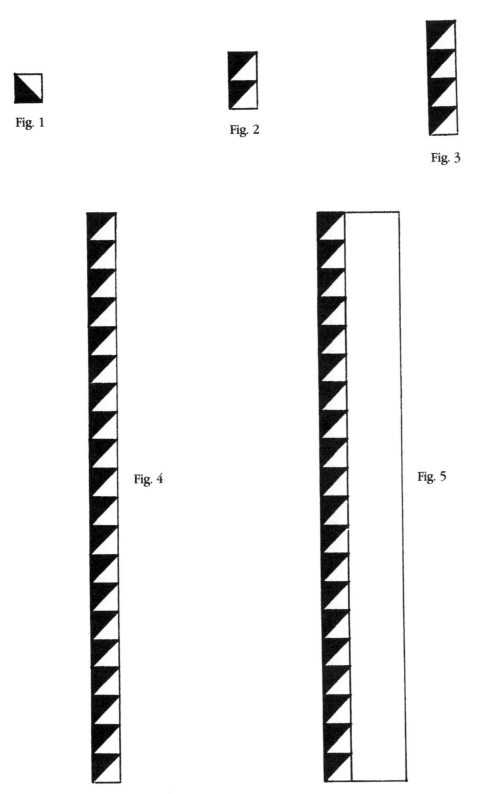

Fig. 1

Fig. 2

Fig. 3

Fig. 4

Fig. 5

PUSS IN THE CORNER

Finished size of quilt: 17″ × 22″.

Finished size of block: 4″ square.

Number of blocks in quilt: 12.

Number of pieces to cut for each block:
    B—four light, four dark.
    M—one light.
    P—four dark.

Templates used: B, M and P.

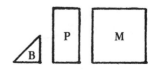

Short lattice: Finished size, 1″ × 4″. Cut eleven 1½″ × 4½″ dark strips.

Long lattice: Finished size: 1″ × 5″. Cut six 1½″ × 5½″ dark strips.

Side borders: Finished size, 1½″ × 19″. Cut two 1¾″ × 19½″ dark strips.

Top and bottom borders: Finished size, 1½″ × 17″. Cut two 1¾″ × 17″ dark strips.

The block is constructed in three horizontal rows. Sew the light and dark B triangles together in pairs to form squares (*Fig. 1*). For the first and third rows, sew a pieced square to each end of a P rectangle (*Fig. 2*). For the second row, sew a P rectangle to opposite sides of an M square (*Fig. 3*). Sew the three rows together to complete the block (*Fig. 4*).

The quilt top is assembled in four rows of three blocks each. For the first row, sew a short lattice strip to one edge of a block (*Fig. 5*); sew a long lattice strip to the lower edge (*Fig. 6*). Repeat with a second block. Sew a short lattice strip to the lower edge of a third block. Sew the three blocks together as in *Fig. 7* to complete the row. Make two more rows the same. For the last row, sew three blocks together with short lattice strips between as in *Fig. 8*. Sew the four rows together. Sew the borders to the sides, then to the top and bottom of the quilt top.

In the quilt shown on the inside front cover, we have added a single corner block. To make this block, cut one light and one dark triangle, using Template Y. Sew the triangles together to form a square. Cut 1½″ off one end of the bottom border and sew on the pieced square. Sew the border to the quilt.

Finish the quilt following the General Instructions.

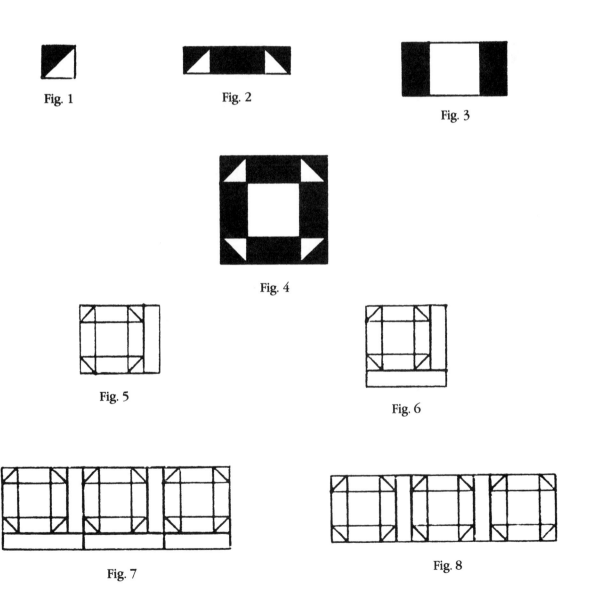

Fig. 1   Fig. 2   Fig. 3

Fig. 4

Fig. 5   Fig. 6

Fig. 7   Fig. 8

ANNA'S CHOICE VARIATION

Finished size of quilt: 13½″ × 17½″.

Finished size of block: 4″ square.

Number of blocks in quilt: Four.

Number of pieces to cut for each block:
B—16 light, 16 dark.

Lattice strips: Finished size, 2″ × 4″. Cut eight light strips 2½″ × 4½″.

Corner pinwheels: Finished size, 2″ square. Cut 12 light B triangles and 12 dark B triangles.

Templates used: B.

Side borders: Finished size, 1¾″ × 14″. Cut two light strips 2″ × 14½″.

Top and bottom borders: Finished size, 1¾″ × 13½″. Cut two light strips 2″ × 13½″.

Each block is constructed in four horizontal rows. First, sew the light and dark B triangles together in pairs to form squares (*Fig. 1*). Sew these squares together to form four rows of four squares each as in *Fig. 2*. Carefully matching the seams, sew rows 1 and 2 together to form a rectangle (*Fig. 3*). Repeat with rows 3 and 4 (*Fig. 4*). Sew the two rectangles together to complete the block (*Fig. 5*).

Make three corner pinwheels by sewing four pieced squares together for each one as in *Fig. 6*.

Assemble the quilt top in five horizontal rows. For rows 1, 3 and 5, sew a lattice strip to opposite sides of a corner pinwheel (*Fig. 7*). For rows 2 and 4, sew a block to opposite sides of a lattice strip (*Fig. 8*). Sew the rows together, carefully matching the seams. Sew on the side, then the top and bottom borders.

Finish the quilt following the General Instructions.

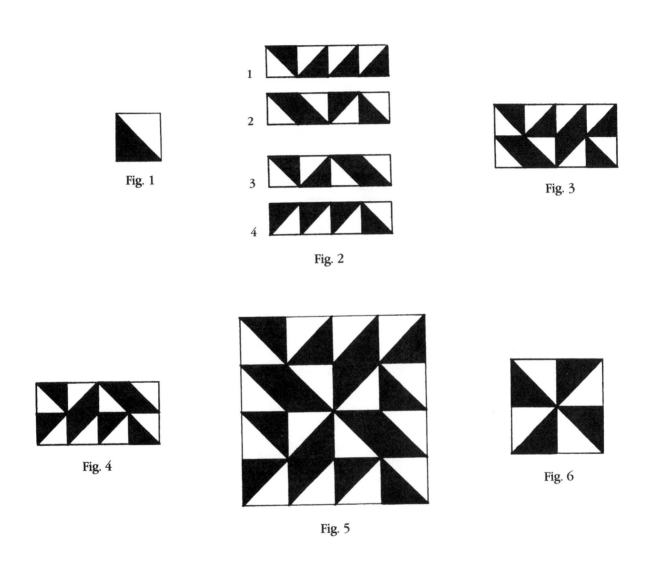

Fig. 1

Fig. 2

Fig. 3

Fig. 4

Fig. 5

Fig. 6

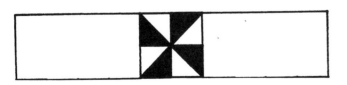

Fig. 7

Fig. 8

JACOB'S LADDER

Finished size of quilt: 16½″ × 20½″.

Finished size of block: 4″ square.

Number of blocks in quilt: 12.

Number of pieces to cut for each block:
F—two color, two white.
J—four color, four white.

Corner block: Finished size, 2″ square. Cut eight white and eight colored J squares.

Side borders: Finished size, 2″ × 16″. Cut two 2½″ × 16½″ strips of white.

Top and bottom borders: Finished size, 2″ × 12″. Cut two 2½″ × 12½″ strips of white.

For each block, sew a colored F triangle to a white F triangle to make a square (*Fig. 1*). Sew two white and two colored J squares together as in *Fig. 2* to form a larger square. Sew these two pieced squares together to form a rectangle (*Fig. 3*). Repeat to form a second rectangle, then sew the two rectangles together to complete the block (*Fig. 4*).

Templates used: F and J.

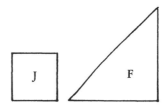

Arrange the blocks in four rows of three blocks each, making sure that all of the blocks are turned in the same direction. Sew the blocks in each row together, then sew row 1 to row 2 and row 3 to row 4. Sew the pairs of rows together. Sew the borders to the sides.

For each corner block, sew two white and two colored J squares together as for the block. Sew a corner block to each end of the top and bottom borders. Sew the borders to the quilt top.

Finish the quilt following the General Instructions.

Fig. 1

Fig. 2

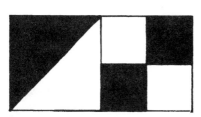

Fig. 3

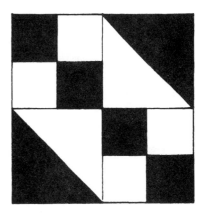

Fig. 4

NINE PATCH

Finished size of quilt: 16″ × 21½″.

Finished size of block: 4½″ square.

Number of blocks in quilt: 12.

Number of pieces to cut for each block:
J—four color.
N—one color.
Q—four white.

Corner square: Finished size, 1″ square. Cut six colored J squares.

Lattice: Finished size, 1¼″ × 4½″. Cut 17 strips 1½″ × 5″ of white.

The block is constructed in three horizontal rows. For rows 1 and 3, sew a small J square to each end of a Q rectangle (*Fig. 1*). For row 2, sew a Q rectangle to opposite sides of a large N square (*Fig. 2*). Sew the

Templates used: J, N and Q.

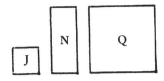

three rows together to complete the block (*Fig. 3*).

Assemble the quilt top in seven horizontal rows. For rows 1, 3, 5 and 7, sew three blocks together with lattice strips between (*Fig. 4*). For rows 2, 4 and 6, sew three lattice strips together with corner squares between (*Fig. 5*). Sew row 1 to 2, 3 to 4, and 5 to 6. Sew the pairs of rows together; sew row 7 to the lower edge.

Finish the quilt following the General Instructions.

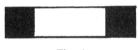

Fig. 1

Fig. 2

Fig. 3

Fig. 4

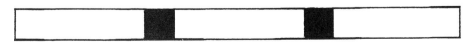

Fig. 5

SUGAR BOWL

Templates used: C, G, K and R.

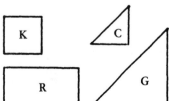

Finished size of quilt: 17¼″ × 22¼″.

Finished size of block: 5″ square.

Number of blocks in quilt: Four.

Number of pieces to cut for each block:
  C—six white, six dark.
  G—one white, one dark.
  K—one white, one dark.
  R—two white.

Lattice strips: Finished size, 1¼″ × 5″. Cut four 1¾″ × 5½″ strips of white.

Center square: Finished size, 1¼″ square. Cut one dark K square.

Inner top and bottom borders: Finished size, 1¼″ × 11¼″. Cut two 1¾″ × 11¾″ strips of white.

Sawtooth borders: Finished size, 1¼″ × 11¼″. Cut 18 white and 18 dark C triangles.

Side borders: Finished size, 3″ × 16¼″. Cut two 3¼″ × 16¾″ strips of white.

Outer top and bottom borders: Finished size, 3″ × 17¼″. Cut two 3¼″ × 17¼″ strips of white.

Sew the dark triangles to the white triangles to form squares (*Fig. 1*). For each block, sew two small pieced squares together as in *Fig. 2*. Sew this piece to one side of the large pieced square as in *Fig. 3*. Sew two small pieced squares and one dark K square together to form a strip as in *Fig. 4*; sew this strip to the top of the previous piece (*Fig. 5*). Sew a small pieced square to one end of an R rectangle (*Fig. 6*); sew this strip to the side edge of the piece (*Fig. 7*). Following *Fig. 8*, sew a small pieced square to the end of the remaining R rectangle; sew a white K square to the other side of the pieced square. Sew this strip to the lower edge of the block to complete it (*Fig. 9*).

The quilt top is assembled in horizontal rows. For rows 1 and 2, sew the blocks together in pairs with a lattice strip between as in *Fig. 10*. For row 2, sew the center square to one end of a lattice strip, sew the remaining lattice strip to the other side of the center square. Arrange the three rows so that all of the dark K squares are at the center. Sew row 2 to 1, then sew row 3 to row 2. Sew on the inner top and bottom borders.

For each sawtooth border, sew nine small pieced squares together to form a strip (*Fig. 11*). Sew these borders to the top and bottom of the quilt top. Sew on the side borders, then the outer top and bottom borders.

Finish the quilt following the General Instructions.

Fig. 1   Fig. 2   Fig. 3

Fig. 4

Fig. 5

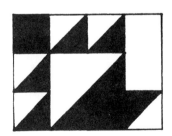

Fig. 6   Fig. 7

Fig. 8

Fig. 9

Fig. 10

Fig. 11

X-QUISITE

Finished size of quilt: 17″ × 19½″.

Finished size of block: 2½″ square.

Number of blocks in quilt: 42.

Number of pieces to cut for each block:
C—two dark.
W—one white.

Side borders: Finished size, 1″ × 17½″. Cut two 1¼″ × 18″ strips of white.

Top and bottom borders: Finished size, 1″ × 17″. Cut two 1¼″ × 17″ strips of white.

For each block, sew a C triangle to each diagonal edge of the W wedge (*Fig. 1*). Keeping the triangles at the upper left and lower right of each block, arrange the blocks in seven rows of six blocks each. Sew the blocks together to form the rows, then sew the rows together

in pairs, carefully matching the seamlines; you will have one row of blocks left over. Sew the pairs together; sew the "extra" row to the bottom edge.

Sew the borders to the sides, then to the top and bottom of the quilt top.

Finish the quilt following the General Instructions.

Templates used: C and W.

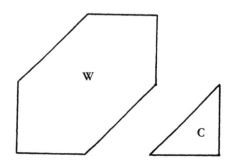

Fig. 1

QUILTING PATTERNS

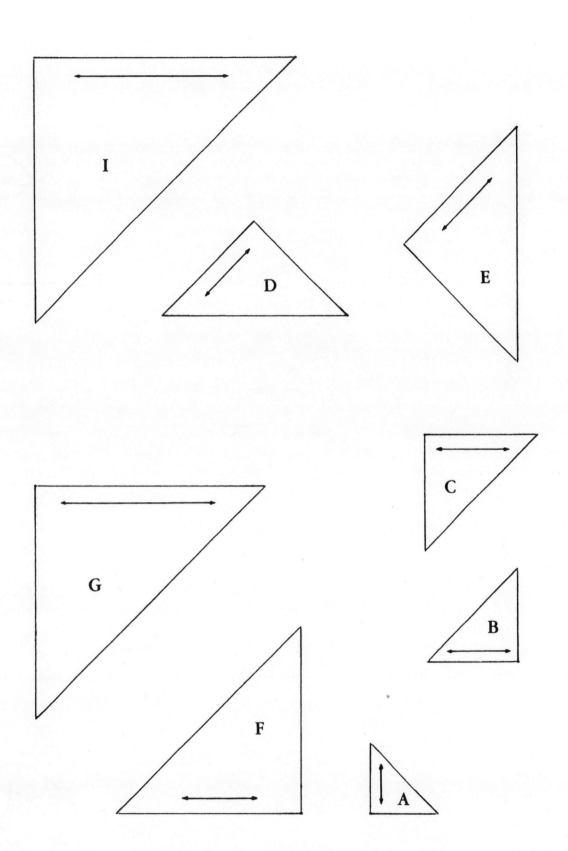

Add ¼″ seam allowance around all edges.　　　　PLATE 1

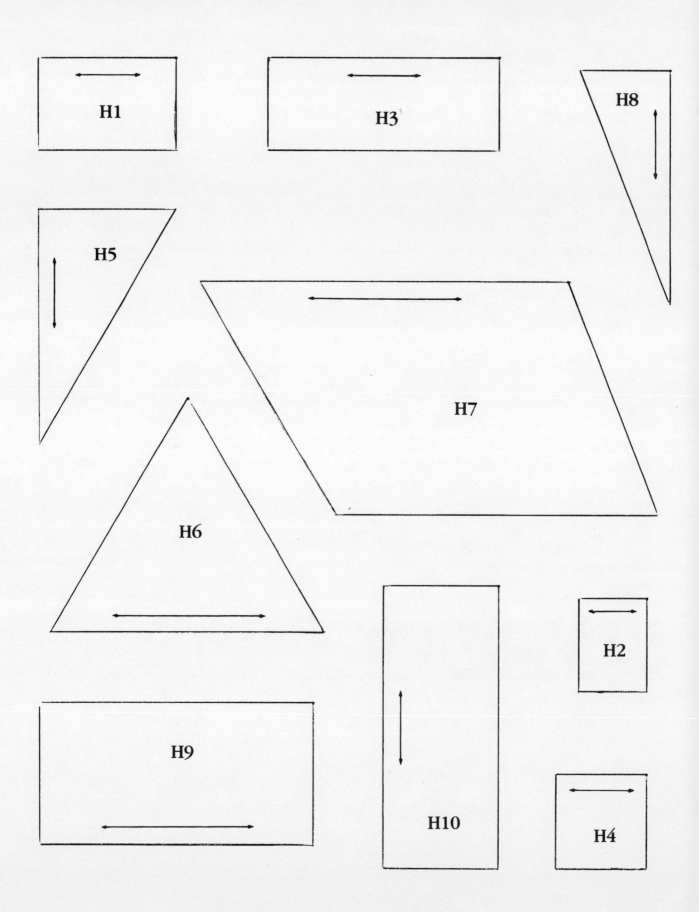

PLATE 2

Add ¼″ seam allowance around all edges.

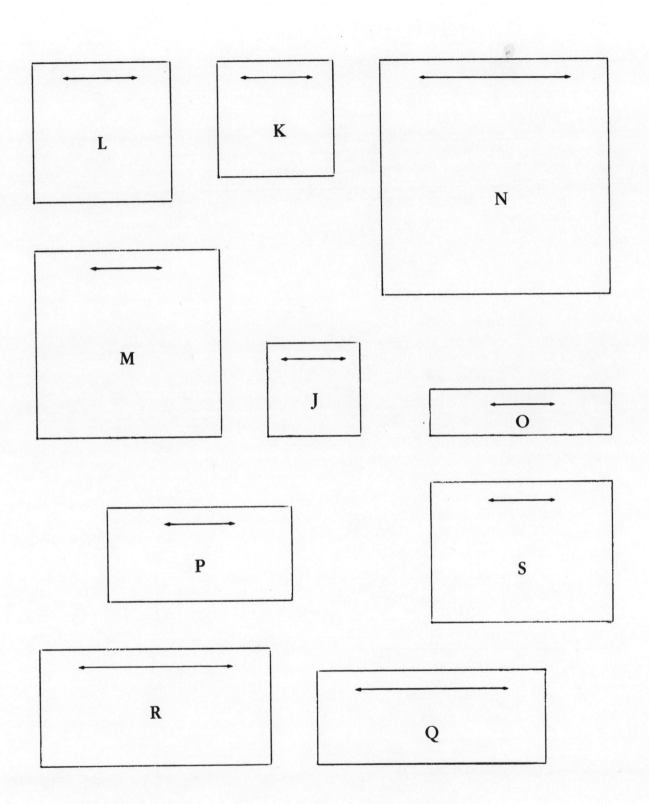

Add ¼″ seam allowance around all edges.

PLATE 3

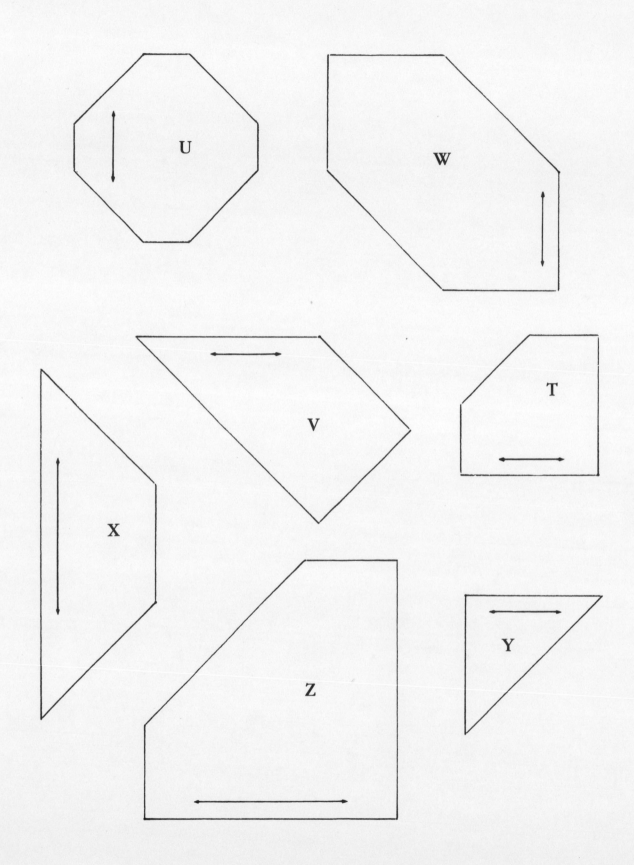

PLATE 4

Add ¼″ seam allowance around all edges.